FLIGHTS OF THE
HARVEST-MARE
by
Linda Bierds

Linda Bierds (signature)

Ahsahta Press

Boise State University
Boise, Idaho

Some of these poems first appeared in the following magazines and anthologies: *Anthology of Magazine Verse and Yearbook of American Poetry, Backbone, Black Warrior Review, Chomo-Uri, Chowder Review, Cutbank, The Fiddlehead, Hudson Review, Jeopardy, Massachusetts Review, New Letters, Poetry Northwest, Porch, Quarterly West, Seattle Review, Swallow's Tale, Wind,* and *Xanadu.*

Editor for Ahsahta Press: Dale K. Boyer

ISBN 0-916272-27-3
Library of Congress Catalog Card Number:
84-73272

For Sydney

Contents

Part One

Part Two

Part Three

Introduction

From Oregon to South Africa, Italy to Brooklyn, the mid-west to Wales—in houses, fields, water, caverns, air, or within the borders of particular paintings or biography, Linda Bierds tells the stories of transformations. Often, she reinvents their rituals, and because the poems of **Flights of the Harvest-Mare** so deeply *honour* others' experiences as well as those of the poet, these occasions of the human spirit are specific and fully alive. Bierds' empathy of imagination rises vividly in a poem like "Lost," where the poet describes her dying mother speaking of her own mother's death. It's Brooklyn, 1922, and Bierds' mother is at the cinema, in between worlds. Ready for propitiation, she is compelled towards a close-up of the star:

> *I just swelled from my seat like steam, pressing*
> *that face. Not a kiss, but smoke, like smoke, like*
> *my mouth was that cone of dusty air*
> *from projector to screen.*

Walking home, the ordinary evening becomes hallucinatory, and the poet's mother is suddenly emptied, lost. She falters until the fact of what's occurred

> *. . . latched on, of course. Some*
> *finger of comprehension*
> *lifted its clear bone—*
>
> *And gave me my grief,* she said, and turned
> and homed us, one with the other.

In telling her mother's story, the poet also relives and receives it.

"Lost" is indicative of a strategy dear to Bierds' poetic impulses: confluent episodes that become cyclical in their final emphasis. This is one way, along with her range of subjects, that Bierds cannily avoids static, over-personal, or sentimental gestures. Narrative or emotional situations become heightened by images that are not quite familiar but have their happy place in what's required to proceed towards resolution. With accurate perception, staggered and surprising, her rhythms carry a swift sluicing music to engage the reader, as here in the first half of one of Bierds' loveliest poems, "Zuñi Potter: Drawing the Heartline":

> Through the scratch strokes of piñon,
> arroyos, through the clamped earth
> waxed and swollen,
> coil to coil, paddle to anvil,

the bowl on her palm-skin blossoms,
the bowl on her lap
blossoms, the lap blossoms

in its biscuit of bones.

Through repetitive syntax and the tension of sibilance and liquidity, these lines work as an incantation which both lulls and startles. One becomes part of the process of shaping the bowl and its significant decoration; the potter and the artifact are joined in a final perfect form. And so too is the reader, until the concluding image of release:

. . . she sketches an arrow,
its round path nostril to heart.
For the breath going in.
For the breath going out.
Wind to heartbeat. The blossoms of steam.

Without denying facts, without allowing memory and assessment to become simplistic, Bierds writes of what is mysterious and elemental, even holy. Such elusive states can be lovely, but they are often baffling, even, sometimes, monstrous. The power and threat in "Mid-Plains Tornado" is relentlessly physical:

Think of teeth being drilled, that enamel and blood
burning circles inside your cheek. That's like the fury.
Only now it's quail and axles, ...

It's with you all morning. Something wet in the air.
Sounds coming in at a slant, like stones
clapped under water. And pigs, slow to the trough.

An ominous build-up, discomfort headed for pain, or worse. Not until the third and final stanza does the speaker really join the scene. To take this knowledge within her, she must break through the membrane of her own horror:

The last time, I walked a fresh path toward the river.
Near the edge of a field I found our mare, pierced
through the side by the head of her six-week foal.
Her ribs, her great folds of shining skin
closed over the skull. I watched them forever it seemed:
eight legs, two necks, one astonished head curved
back in a little rut of hail. And across the river
slim as a road, a handful of thrushes set down
in an oak tree, like a flurry of leaves

drawn back again.

And so Bierds resolves the indifferent brutality suffered by both the horses and herself by moving her perspective beyond, up to the birds so that she might accept a world that, in some form, will bear such violence again.

Bierds' poems clearly apprehend the nature of mystery; they offer a vivid suspension within a larger, inaccessible knowledge. What Bierds releases is momentarily certain, which is as certain as one can truly be. Hers is a forceful imagination, one which makes stunning connections, as in the poem "In Prague, In Montmarte." It's 1874, and two scientists in Prague are, just that moment, excitedly on the verge of a discovery in genetics:

> Can it be these filaments, these
> couple-beads, distinguish us? Nostril? Nail?

Simultaneously, in Paris, Degas is backing away to regard a canvas where ballerinas ready themselves:

> . . . the cumbersome, full
> bodies, the music, full, delayed but a moment
> like the dragged note of the milktrain,
> just passing—in Prague, in Montmarte—

> Yes, he whispers, to no one.

The poem is about that instant, *is* that instant, when something becomes suddenly, perfectly clear. A difficult matter to describe, for once a poem's experience is resolved, one must begin all over again with the small, or large, knowledge of what has been tenuously gained.

The questing spirit which answers something in all of us is the concern of this book. Bierds' choices of who and what to write about, their diversity, bring this spirit alive. Remarkable in a first volume, we know the poems while the poet remains elusive. I find this refreshing and provocative in the wake of innumerable books where one knows all too much of the poet-as-person's daily habits and neuroses. **Flights of the Harvest-Mare** is a work of sustaining character; it explores far beyond a single dooryard and, in so doing, encounters deep and disturbing spirit and world.

Pamela Stewart
St. Ives, Cornwall

I am not one, as you think, but two.

from Frazer's **The Golden Bough**

Part One

Guide in a Glowworm Cave

Everyone has sung here: Dame Nellie Melba, Gracie Fields,
the Vienna Boys Choir. All scuffling down the stairs
just like you, with the river gnawing beneath the planks.
Just look at this limestone cathedral, this organ,
its smooth, white pipes. I swear when you sing
those pipes will hum it back. And the Wedding
Party. See how the bride kneels against the rail.
Each year she bows a little lower, as water drips,
and the priest slopes over his blessing.

I know you're cold, but those aren't icicles
over our heads—they're roots. And this is their earth
we are under. In time they will reach these planks.
It will be like walking through a harp then,
and then it will all close over.

But now to the boat. Don't make a sound.
I'll pull us along by a rope on the ceiling,
through these black tunnels of water . . . and there they are:
a million tiny lights: a heaven, of course, the warm stars.

Sometimes at night when I bring the boat back
I reach up and touch their foodlines, like eyelashes
on my fingers, and I think of those worms reeling in,
taking a crisp midge and my salt into their round mouths,
and I sing out one sharp note and watch their lights
sheathe over. It's beautiful then! That note
humming around these walls, and just a hundred worms
still glowing out the Dippers, the Milky Way,
and so close I'm almost there.

Saving

*—The six-year-old slipped through the
well shaft in Frascati, 15 miles from Rome.
—AP*

*Down through the top dirt, the stone pocks,
loose roots and clam-earth, one hundred, tapering,
two hundred feet, this child, Alfredo, falling,
pin-hipped and silent, falling,
lodging at last where the scratch-tube opens.*

And here, at that moment, the surface:
cypress, bluewood, an acre of foxglove,
one hencote, one lean-to, one woman
turning, just turning.

You move your neck and your good arm,
look up, look
up, and there, everything, cypress and hencote,
condensed to a star.

Alfredo, when the star blunts out it is evening.
Now the other, far
beyond . . . it is night.

*   *   *

One day, then two.
I read there are currents just under you,
longer than Italy. I think
of an hour-glass:
the funnel from sky to earth,
the waist where your body struggles,
the funnel beneath you reopening,

how each of us, feeling this,
waits with you.

*   *   *

This morning, just after your death,
I am climbing a hill to the city.
Two people beside me are speaking of you,
the unbearable rivers still sucking your heels.
We must save him, one says. One
closes his eyes as just for a moment
the linked bones of your body rush under us.

*   *   *

We will lift you.
For motion, for the stratifications of light,
we will give you our words, our
ceremonies:
One bell must pulse from its sleek dome.
One woman, long watching, must sing.

Mirror

Before the mirror, water gave it
back, the brown surface of another's eye.

*

It is High South Africa, 1630.
A rabble of sailors press down the Zambize.
Now, strewn out through their empty camp:
burlap, fig stones, and this—
this oblong, black-backed glass.

*

Clear night. The first creep in
from the bushwood, sifting.
This is my face, one whispers. A flush
like a thud in the brain. *This is my face,
unrippled. Its pockets and stains. Its long
surprise.*

A mynah calls in her seven voices:
Aye Aye Aye Aye . . .

Something lifts up through the mangroves.
Something sets in.

Source

—All of the crimes were traced to the victim.
—AP

What did you call to that day in the paddock,
your child's brain clear of its judgement? He turned
to whatever sin ignored you, saw you slim
in your britches, saw your hand
lift to your hat brim, the breast-hub lift,

and he rose from the calf at his knees—quickly—
all in one motion—like steam through an opening
window—then running, waving the iron, chased you
fifty, a hundred, two hundred feet

and branded you high on the back-thigh:

the britches melting, the skin puckered and sucked,
two worms of flame, the pain a fuchsia light
in your eyes, a bell in your ears, and the mind
turning. Already turning.

    S with a little s inside. Double S. Circle Ss.
    A hiss on the back-thigh, you fingered
    and grew. Your children grew.
    Your body turned from its making, rested,
    husk-thin, drying, the S and little s
    less than a whisper.

What did you witness to start this again?
Brief, something brief? A man lifting his hand
in a wave? A cane lifted? Smoke curling up
from a flannel sleeve?

You sit at the round table. Slowly you trace
the small shape of your name. Write Ruth
you are evil. Write Ruth your britches are
candles. Source. Inciter.
The pull and push of your long hand, the letters
flames at your fingers.

The Haunting

In the night you dream of ovens—
flame vaults,
piece by piece, snuffing me back.
Without hands, now, without arms,
I weave through your dreams like a salmon.
If the moon is right I can watch you grieve for me.

Here in a field I rename the world:
hawthorn, foxglove, leopardbane.
If you hear me at all,
I am only a pulse, a lapping of water.

Above us a plane carves random letters,
crisp as porcelain.
They initial us. They initial the meadow,
the headwater, the salmon in its
trough of eggs and gravel.

They are the smoke of your dreams.

A Walk in Early Autumn

*—Near-death experiences are surprisingly
similar: an unpleasant noise, a tunnel,
a beckoning light . . . often a guide.*

It is evening and you will come
no further with me than the first corner:
The fog is too heavy; it appears to be raining.
I watch you fade up the hill.

There is no water on this road;
I touch my dry shoulders.
Only the trees rain.

Near the ravine, blackberries pock the bushes.
Their sparse fur captures the water, the early mold.
Over-ripe, they collapse in my palm
like warming igloos.

I touch my head;
the only rain is falling from the fir branches.
There are no circles in the puddles and
there is no sound, just the tree rain
and the stark ratchet of a crow.

A large dog has pressed through the hedge.
It follows along the shoulder path,
stopping when I stop. It does not
enter the road. We travel together a mile,
starting, stopping, like a small train.

When it spins back to the forest I watch
its thin legs prance.

Look, here is the warm glow of the house.

Lost

Once, not long from her own death, my mother spoke
of her mother: moribund, so sharp with disease,
a splinter, she said, day after day
working down through the fleshy bed.

*I was just fourteen. I would sit, watching
her parts, her wrists and renegade knuckles.*

It was Easter, 1922. In the late afternoon
an aunt, chastened with Christ, came calling.
And my mother, free in the dusk-light! Oh Brooklyn,
your coupes and roadsters. Your fox-scarves!
Down Fulton, down Bedford and Smith to
the Brooklyn Strand, the cropped seats, ten seconds
of twilight, of full night, a flicker, the beam
and Talmadge's face flashed like the first sun.

*I just swelled from my seat like steam, pressing
that face. Not a kiss, but smoke, like smoke, like
my mouth was that cone of dusty air
from projector to screen.*

My mother, half in the film, half in the cool
night, walked along Smith Street, past stoops,
past Christs and flannel rabbits dim
in the storefronts. Then she turned full face
to the street, saw the asphalt, the lamplights,
saw the sleek-sided roadsters, and *lifted,*

lost, up from her shoulders, her chemise
and long shoes. Lost, she faltered in
terrible circles: the dumb body, its cloud of
self, the stoops taking back their patterns,
the white hands tapping, again and again,
the hat-bud, the ears.

*Until something latched on, of course. Some
finger of comprehension
lifted its clear bone—*

And gave me my grief, she said, and turned
and homed us, one with the other.

Fur Traders
Descending the Missouri: 1845

—from the painting by George Caleb Bingham

In the year this painting was lived,
genre as it is, without
innuendo,
the snowmelt had lifted the river;
the April buffaloes, long drowned in the flooding,
were moving still, in the muscles,
in the heartlobes of buzzards.

It is late afternoon, late August.
We focus first on a fox, chained
to the prowlift,
and then, behind, on a Sioux-French
boy, and then, behind,
on the helmsman.
The sense of peace is unending,
the balance of harvest.
Just off on the shoreline, the raptors,
the foxes, the brushgrass and hunters
take from each other.
This is not a painting

of grief.
This is not a painting that asks
for our grief.
A boy leans back toward his father.
A fox watches its shadow.
The fuchsia half-light moves with the river.

Ritual for the Dead,
Lake Sakami, Quebec, 1980

The moose has fallen smoothly, without sound,
lifting her head only once
from a tangle of sweet-grass and snow.
Now the Cree lower their greased rifles.
Kneeling against the cold, they open the stomach,
the tendons and black muscles, and now
two calves are peeled from the steaming womb:

> Their skulls are heavy. Their thin bodies
> glisten. They lie in the snow
> like the parallel arms of a child.

Slowly, two flaps of meat are sliced
from the mother's flank. The mouths
of the calves are opened. Now the salty flaps
ooze in their jaws like tongues. And now,
through the cold palms of the hunters,
through their stroking, shivering voices,
the dead throats are stirring,
the stomachs and hearts are stirring,
the brains are stirring
as they glaze through the dim eyes:

> *This is the promise of sunrise,*
> *of harvest, of winter*
> *cracking from our tight bellies.*
> *This is the promise of blood.*
> *Swallow.*

Grandson

Your grandmother has not moved from her couch
for twenty days. On a table near her arm are bottles
of soft pills, and a cup of water, pierced
by a curved glass straw. She rests in afghans
she crocheted a decade earlier. Often now
she thinks of birds weaving their own protections,
from hair and string, from pale, curling roots.

You have met one another just twice before.
Once she cut a slingshot from the branch
of a plum tree, her loose dress curling
past the knees of elastic stockings,
her rough shoes heeling the trunk.
And once, in the haze of a taffeta lampshade,
she lowered her black hair.
How it stretched down her back, wild and electric!

Now you bend to her hands, to the taut amber skin
of her forehead. And now her breathing guides you
as you nod by the window . . .
the crickets are grinding,
the plum tree shivers again.
You are running down a country road,
dormant muscles pumping, arms lifting—
and you are racing through a prairie of wild grass.
At your side a slim black horse gallops across your shadow.

You will run together: where barns are sloping,
where fat cicadas are clicking like stars.

Kinderspelen

—from the painting by Bruegel

As your peasants dance in their grave frenzies,
your grim-eyed bridesmaids plant and glide,
as your pipers stare out past their droning—

here, full reign through a township, two hundred
children tumble their hoops, their jacks and nine-pins.
With somber compulsion, they will play!
Knuckles, leap-frog, Whom-shall-I-marry,
the marriage—the mime—the Whitsun child-bride
folded in silence. Two hundred children—
elbow to thigh to stilt to pig-back to

this, high at the left and fading:
A pasture. A river. A boy, naked,
swims out from the jitter. A boy
shinnies the crisp aspen. And

the courtyards are filling, the store-fronts
and portals. Two boys push out from the bankside.
Two girls twirl in their red skirts—twirl
faster—and there, by the river, by the tops
and pin-wheels, the skirts are lifting, the skirts
are filling, the air is filling—
now music, the voices—hoop-whistle, whinny—
now the girls drop through the red billows:

One sun. *Another!*

The Poppies

—after the painting by Monet

—   *Whatever is made*
The object of your vision is so made
Because another is looking at it too,
A fraction of a second earlier.
                    Howard Nemerov

At last a fragile light, hazing the poplars
and peaked red roofs. You roll from your cave of blankets,
take tea and steaming ham—then off to the fields
with little Jean dancing behind. How easily he forgives you,
that blanketed back curved to the wall.

And here is Camille, lifting her arm
to match a graceful stride.
She is just descending a shallow hill blazing with poppies.
Her open blue parasol slips from her shoulder
and rests—there—where the white muscles of her upper arm
meet and divide. As she walks you watch pale foxtails
lapping the hem of her skirt . . . and then at her elbow
Jean with his red bouquet: How the stems are thick in his fists,
how they drop now and then, a bead of milky sap.

All morning clouds interrupt the sun.
You pause in this alternate light, think of Jean and Camille
at the crest of the hill, think of slanting fields,
of poppies bobbing like scarlet birds:

And there, at the crest of the hill, is another woman
and another boy: The child's arms are empty.
The woman scans the bending grass.

Now she draws from the folds of her skirt
a sheathed blue umbrella.

Now the boy is filling his arms with flowers.

And Jean and Camille approach you, smelling of purslane
and clover. Jean lifts his arms:

16

Your gifts, your poppies, come flaming.

One Hot Day in October

You wait in a corner of the schoolyard,
damp in your peppered cords.
At last, down soft, sucking asphalt
your father's car comes shimmering toward you.

You have never been swimming together
and you sing down the country roads,
past barns and withering pumpkins.
His collar is open.
His false teeth curve in his pocket
like the hoof of a tiny horse.

You walk through madronna leaves to the harbor.

In the shadow of a huge stone
you turn from each other.
When you look again, his skin
is the color of sliced pears.
His bathing suit is deep
blue wool, with a belt, and a buckle
where a slim woman arcs in a swan dive.

He dives through the water.
His hair flows from his head like kelp.
He is turning. He is kicking
and stroking with a smooth, terrible
grace you have never seen.
He is the sea for you.
He is the pelican lurching
through a long, white sky.
You will swim in his wake forever.

Part Two

Tongue

—I did not know that my fingers were spelling
a word, or even that words existed.
—Helen Keller

Imagine another,
blind, deaf since birth.
One, nearly two, she squats at the lip
of a shallow pond. Above her,
the day exchanges its sunlight, clouds.
This she feels in blushes across her shoulders.

With a sleepwalker's grope
she is reaching, patting the cold grasses,
and now, from a tangle of water cardinals
she has plucked a pond-snail. Moist and shell-less

it sucks across her palm.
Tongue, she senses, the simile
wordless, her fingers tracing the plump muscle,
the curling tip.
Someone approaches. To the bowl
of her free hand, the name is spelled
the tingling *sn* and *ail.*
Again. Again.

And soon she will learn. The naming.
The borders of self,
other. But for now, propped in the musky
shoregrass, it is tongue she senses,
as if the snail, mute, in the lick
of its earthy foot,
contained a story. As if her hand
received it.

Emanuela

They prepare me, speaking in tongues.
Mother. My father and brother.
They sway. They churn from their soft shoes.

Still,
like the boll I am waiting, like the husk
curved to its blossom.

Now the bishop is chanting,
pressing my temples. His forearms
are stiff and glisten. His throat is
stiff in its backlash of tendons.
Open he calls, pressing my temples.
Receive he is calling, pressing *Receive*
I am rocking, his rake and shimmer,
Receive I am rocking *Receive Receive.*
And now at the heart-bone words are forming
lo and sha   lo and sha   rising   rising
wind   the hissle and long
push   break   break   SIA SIA SIA SIA
The gift he is calling   I do not
know *Holy Holy*   I do not know
my parents are moving beside me like
flames   their beautiful arms
lifting like flames   their faces
are wet they are candles beside me
Cristo Cristo   I know I know I
know but the thousand words for song

Zuñi Potter:
Drawing the Heartline

Through the scratch-strokes of piñon, the hissing
arroyos, through the clamped earth
waxed and swollen,
coil to coil, paddle to anvil,
the bowl on her palm-skin blossoms,
the bowl on her lap
blossoms, the lap blossoms

in its biscuit of bones.
Bract-flower, weightless, in the pock and shimmer
of August, she slopes from the plumegrass like
plumegrass. And the white skull
bobbles and turns. The gingerroot fingers
turn. Through the cocked mouth
of a buck deer, she sketches an arrow,
its round path nostril to heart.
For the breath going in.
For the breath going out.
Wind to heartbeat. The blossoms of steam.

From the Great Depression

It is a trick the poor pass down, this
dipping of sweaters, until the wool itself
sucks down through the sizes, and the children
turn in the doorways, winter-ready in perfect fits.
(But for the monograms, full and puckered, pinched
over their hearts like the feet of crows. . . .)

And accepting this trick, a woman
leans to a kettle. Steam
curls past her shoulders, past
the magazine snapshot of Christ
tacked over the woodstove—the beautiful one,
where he gazes far off to the left, like
a soft-eyed Jack of Diamonds anyone might draw.
First you are tired, she thinks, then
the throat closes over. The membrane,
gray as a kettle, grows, closes.
The sound the dipthetic makes—the stridor—

is the sound of a cart over ice furrows,

the children tumbling out at the schoolyard, with
the black germs of their laughter
simply vapor on the snow.
All winter, slumped in their perfect rows, they learn
of the great repetitions of

peak and valley.
And where is that time, that
peak, the woman wonders. Blue gloves, a ballroom so warm
the eyebrows glisten. She smiles. Sweaters wind
through her arms like boneless swimmers.
A society of grandparents honed down to
initials!—with the names they insist on just
vapor, a passage of breath:

Willa, Louisa, Percival, Neville, Maud, Reginald, Rex.

24

Believing

His wife is dying, just over eighty, embolisms
on the kidneys and the veins gone.
All afternoon, driving home through the scrub oaks
and derricks, he thought of
trout, sluicing the flats, their tug
and weave, the gulf salt wind firm
on his back. Now, or an hour from now,
the phone will ring and she will be dead.
He leaves their small table. Outside,
two boys slip a kayak
through the blunt canal. "Stroke,"
he calls to them, "stroke." They lower
their two-palmed oars. There is silence,
a wake, thin, like a rip on the water.
He moves inside, pulls the phone to the door,
walks back and stares down the bulkhead.
The boys have slid from the channel
to the lip of the coast. He turns
to the house, turns back: Here
is that firm wind, mullet scratching
the slim canal, fresh night
with its moon. Now a child is screaming across
the yards: The dog is snapping.
"Hug its neck," he shouts. Then again,
"Hug its neck." And if he were closer
he would shout it all:
Hug its body—the fur and gristle,
the flipping chin. Hug it high and tight
through your arms. Until it stops hating.

Mid-Plains Tornado

I've seen it drive straw straight through a fence post—
sure as a needle in your arm—the straws all erect
and rooted in the wood like quills.
Think of teeth being drilled, that enamel and blood
burning circles inside your cheek. That's like the fury.
Only now it's quail and axles, the northeast bank
of the Cedar River, every third cottonwood.

It's with you all morning. Something wet in the air.
Sounds coming in at a slant, like stones
clapped under water. And pigs, slow to the trough.
One may rub against your leg, you turn with a kick
and there it is, lurching down from a storm cloud:
the shaft pulses toward you across the fields
like a magician's finger.
You say goodbye to it all then, in a flash over
your shoulder, with the weathervane so still
it seems painted on the sky.

The last time, I walked a fresh path toward the river.
Near the edge of a field I found our mare, pierced
through the side by the head of her six-week foal.
Her ribs, her great folds of shining skin
closed over the skull. I watched them forever it seemed:
eight legs, two necks, one astonished head curved
back in a little rut of hail. And across the river
slim as a road, a handful of thrushes set down
in an oak tree, like a flurry of leaves
drawn back again.

The Genius of
Earlswood Asylum

Darkness, black moth the light burns up in.
                              —Charles Wright

Sometimes in a great while, one
who cannot feed himself, who cannot stop
tapping, will take to his shoulder
a violin, small curved beautiful body,
and play.

It is not rote. It is proven,
it is not rote.

One who cannot hold his
water, draws cats. Sells cats to George
the Fourth. *The Cat's
Raphael.*

Here is your brain, dimpled with fact. Here
are their brains—loam-globes, a groove
for breathing, a groove for
cats, for melody, for the square root
of anything. The geniuses,
the wizards of Earlswood

(blood drawing up from their fingers, their
toes, drawing up to its blue fissure):

Pullen, Earwicker, Alburtus J, and one,
this one, who takes to his center
funerals, who gleans from a book he cannot
read, the names, the ages, the mourners present
for thirty-five, death-filled years.

*Out of the line of burials, he has not
one idea, ᵔot one intelligible reply.*

White fingers, white toes, white
star the dark sucks through.

The Bonecarver, John Eron, Marshalsea Prison, 1760

Well some of us *are* bad. Just that. You look
we are born. You look we are bad. Like pears
flaring from green to liver.
This is our common yard: women, children,
the lily debtors. This is where Clara
waved her tapered feet. *For the King's peace.*

                                        And for ours?
The irons went on—without pain—just cold,
then warm, like the bellies of lizards.

This is our common grave. Each rainfall the bones
push up, purple, white, and then in the sunlight—
mist, and the fresh domes of turnips!

England. Where does it stop? What line
do you cross to be out of England? One field
and a field beyond just the same. When
the keeper turned I would stroke Clara's thigh,
the soft, bald landscape.
Where does it stop? we

laughed. And now, with the others, in that
dark earth where does she stop,
the white lattice their legs make?

First there is rain, and the mist.
There is yard, and a little dip, and then
the grave. In this way, I gather the dead
descending. And they rise to meet me, eager to be
single! Clara, I say

here is a mink with a splinter of black bread,
scratched to the bone with a latch-pin.
And here, a game, the peg-holes, the absolute
borders.
            Clara, when the pegs jump how the mink
shimmies and preens, how the fingers burn,

how the selves swell back through their patterns.
And how we are all dancing, bone-tip to
bone-tip, beast to prancing beast.

Touching the Elephant

—for my brother

You have been inside so long the colors overwhelm you,
and now the elephant is out—
ambling past the hippos and secretary birds,
then down the path toward the honking mules.
All this motion, and these borders of color.

The guard is clipping the big-kneed legs for hoofing
divots in the lawn. A crowd gathers.
You keep shading your eyes with both hands.

Henry,
I should have re-introduced you more slowly.
Here are the first colors: ice,
one slim section of the moon.
And this is motion, this rain enlarging
in the veins of leaves,

the heart of this animal.

We place our palms on the full stomach, the sparse
sharp hairs. Flesh withdraws, then swells
against us. I notice small pebbles and clots of dirt
sprayed through the hairs for insulation.
I notice your hands now, brailling across the hide.

A bland eye rolls.
For a moment the trunk approaches your shoulder
like the arm of an old friend.
And the long breath that touches you
is wind from a cave you remember.

At the Speed of Light

Tourist-plump, the last Oregon dune buggy ambles
off on its elephant wheels.

Blue sky eggs the wind on.
All around us, sand curls into little tornadoes,

hisses, explodes, finally clings
to the black rims of our sunglasses

like circles of infinitesimal stars.
In love with this whiteness, you

clap your hands, tell me the image is lifting,
like a light-strewn pigeon. Intact, you explain,

in a thousand years this hand-swing will break
intact on another planet.

We walk, walk, past tangles of
agate-bright lakes, small and deadly,

their jellied suck-hole shores trembling in the wind.
And then there are only the hills, flat white,

planked at the mid-riff with shadows.
Egypt, I laugh. Ancient Egypt!

And suddenly to each of us a woman
is turning: her sun-blackened feet, her arms,

the brilliant turquoise vessels she
carries—everything—breaking across us.

Dining in the Country

One entire wall is wire mesh.
Above our heads, two slow fans
exchange the heat. Through mesh we watch
a family of peacocks, and beyond
a white bull nodding in slanted wheat.
Your hands encircle your wine glass
with full, blue-tunnelled veins:
I remember how smooth they were,
turning fish hooks and slices
of balsa, on early April mornings.

This room is thick with the sounds
of closing: fans winding down,
peacocks pleading, like dancers
trapped in their glittering costumes.

We walk into early evening,
our feet sinking in cockleburrs
and thick St. Augustine grass.
How beautiful you are: your white
hair and powdered shoes,
your fine linen trousers.
Now a peacock is spreading his train.
Another, smaller, calls again,
from the lowest branch of an oak.

Tapir

Blacker still in this first light,
flat-eyed, pungent,
your trunk and mythic hocks shuddering toward me,
you bring with you

Paraguay. Amazonas. Peru.
That gross and temperate air, thick
with papaya. One toucan
lifting to flames. And again, below,
through ripples of canebreak,
one shadow, huge, centaurian:
Pizarro on horseback, his dark plume nodding. . . .

And that is the way we blossom, two-legged,
checkered in denim, bringing to you from our side
buds we cannot imagine: pure sound, pure
scent—the hipboot, the jawline
gaining shape through a cluster of odors.

Grooming you, taking with toenail and burr,
a little fig, a little green maté,
I speak of the day, the sun's
predictable arc,
the flesh and the spirit,
the abracadabra of stars. . . .
Old beast, I must be the wind for you now,
you are so silent under my hands.

Elegy for 41 Whales Beached in Florence, Oregon June 1979

—There was speculation that a parasite in the whales' ears may have upset their equilibrium and caused them to become disoriented.
                                                        —UPI

In the warm rods of your ears
forty-one parasites hummed
and you came rolling in
like tarred pilings after a hurricane.
What songs were they piping for you?
What promises did you follow, past the coral
and mussels, and out from the frothy hem
of your world?

These are people.
They dance around you now like hooked marlin.
Some are weeping. Some are trying to pull you back.
Some crouch above your blow-holes
and drill their cigarettes into your skin.

All night your teeth are clicking.
All along the beach you are clicking like wind-chimes.
Is the song still piping for you?

This is sand. You cannot swim through it.
These are trees. Those houses on the cliff
are also trees. And the light that blinks
from them now is made from water.
We have a way of reworking the vital:

This is a pit. That was quicklime.
And here is fire.

Part Three

Philter

With the mountains across her back and the wheel
at her elbow, spinning wool browned from the stems
of walnuts, she watched for her first season:
breasts like the hubs of dogwood flowers, blood

that slipped down her banked thighs, cousins
awakened and prodding, uncles and thin brothers
strumming their songs in the buckling cabin.

She bled that fall in a pocket of oak leaves,
squatting, staring. And the wheel, alone in its clearing,
in its tufts of carded wool, threw the black
sloped shadow of a bison.

There was wind and the great head lowered.
Now you begin.

> She lifted their jug from the pantry, dipped
> under her skirt with a dusty hand,
> swirled the sharp, clear blood deep
> in their whiskey. Humming, skimming the floor
> with her turning hem, she whittled a nail
> from her finger: It dropped through the jug
> like a closing eye.

And one of them followed, lugging his rifle,
his heart-strings, his jug with the curling nail.
One rocked in her shivering body.
For her newness, for flesh like a white trout,
for a sky where the old stars crackled,
one of them whispered *My love My love*
while her small heart opened and she
turned her face to the long wall of the forest.

Heat Wave

The killing sun is setting. We leave our withered
horses, our windless, stone-dry wheat,
to come to these lawns, these galleries,
where Nick and Nora and stiff-legged Asta hang
from the sky. Our children are slumped on the grass
like empty jackets. A lung of cicadas
rattles.
        How green we are. How sun
through the elm leaves greens us. How sun
through the windows of celadon vases

greens us. The saxes and trumpets are bleating.
The clays of a thousand years tremble,
regather.
        Oh Nora. Oh Nick with your whiskey,
your ascot, your eye swelling now
like the moon from a hundred miles:
Give us your clear-headed glances.
Skim over our bodies like rain.

Lifting

Each evening near seven, a father lifts
his son—at first without effort, the boy
no more than a swaddle, a sharp interruption
of sleep. Even later, eye to blue
chirruping eye, the son is a bone farm,
all gooseflesh and stubble.

Little by little, everyone grows. Riley
and Junior. Ozzie and Dave. The green nations
stir and toddle. And the son
is still lifted, near middle-age,
his rust-colored wing-tips scratching
the floor, his chest pressed to its
bagpipe's snort—then a kiss and a cuff
and a walk with the moon to his own yard.

Year after year, the son fattens, the father
stoops. One evening, just after seven,
the son is not lifted. Hands knot
at the small of his back, cork soles
stretch and gape, but the son is not lifted.
And where has the energy gone? In that
brief span, nightfall to nightfall, where
has it gone? There was sleep and brunch,
a walk through the terrace, Hearts
and a little chatter. In what
form has the energy gone?
On what spiked back has it lifted?

After Hearing Ernest Gaines

—When you quilt, a lot of times you say "Lord"
as you quilt, just the needle going through,
"Lord." Well it looks like the needle is
saying that.
                    Nora Lee Condra, from the film
                    Quilts in Women's Lives

Near the end of the afternoon, he gave us
this fragment: an aunt, crippled, had raised him.
Flat on her stomach, she slid
through the garden, she slid through the thin
house. And when they had sinned, she sent them—
Ernest, his cousins—to break down the switches
for their own lashings.

Days later, when I take up the statement on quilting
this aunt comes firmly back—nobody's now, just
one of a dozen, a hundred, who lived as they must have
in Kansas, in the scrub pines of West Virginia.

I want her to sew. She sits at the wide table.
The swatches are ready: the birthstar, the briar,
the drowned son's sleeve pinked and blocked.
Notched deep in the cambric, the muse-voice,
thin, coloratura, dips and whispers
Lord, whispers *Lord.* I turn

and she's gone, palming the garden. Someone has
sinned; high in the hackberry, someone is
breaking a slim branch. There is sunlight across
her shoulders, and behind, on the thick wake
of her hips. Now a child is waiting beside her,
stooped for his small pardon. *I want you to*
sew! But the switch-tip is dancing, the boy is
yelping, is laughing, is rolling his back to
the sweetgrass—and she is above him, stretched
thin in her long arc: apron to shoulder to
armbone, now mouth calling *Lord, your forgiveness,*
calling *Lord, your forgiveness,* calling *We*
are your vessels, receive us.

Cactus,
Blossoming Every Hundred Years

A man is kneeling in his canoe.
Over the brittle side he lowers and retrieves and lowers
a clothesline weighted by horseshoes:
for weeks he has sounded the green harbor.
On the shore a crowd cheers as its first bicycle
jiggles along a rutted street. The high
front wheel catches the sun and curls it
out to the man, where he works with his salty line.

All day the wheel spins its yellow arc across the water.

And cheers follow the man, from the beach
through the evergreens
as he carries his boat upside down on his head.
Where the sun crosses his body, his canoe,
the shadow looks like a tomahawk
and the man sees again one young Indian
stooped over the spreading tapestry
of his grandfather's skull.

Then the birds return and the distant, cheering voices.
His house is white in an oval clearing.
His wife and three young daughters are standing together
in the deep mahogany odors of the parlor.
Through the window sunlight warms their pinafores,
their still, black shoes. They are watching a cactus
in a pewter dish, where, for the first time in their lives,
a single blossom lifts its yellow moon.

Dogsled Through the Trees

They will all fit if they slide between one another's knees.
First the man, then the woman, and finally the child,
low slope of a wedge. The woman smooths a sealskin
blanket across the child's lap and whispers:
"Eskimos chew blubber and have teeth like stone."
But the child is thinking of bear rugs, and searches
the blanket for claws, and little marble eyes.

Nine white breaths pant up from the team
of Malamutes, like smoke from an alley of fires.
The animals feel their breast straps tighten, the stiffening tow.
The man feels the Eskimo's knees against his shoulderblades
and the firm saddle of the woman's back.

Now a quick whistle and the sled lurches forward—
and then no sound, no gee or haw, only runners slicing the snow.
Together the man and woman, and the small child,
watch the galloping white rumps of the Malamutes.

Just as the team arcs toward the trees,
a thought freezes in the man's mind,
like a rabbit stunned in a snowy trail
with nine jaws approaching:

"Everyone who carries my father's name is in this sled."

And then the thought is gone.

A crow is lifting from a branch above the sled,
a glistening, black salute.
The man curls his neck and glimpses the pale, flat claws
and brief underbeak. And now the Eskimo's face
on a sky the color of snow. The sharp bones curving
like wings. The sharp, black eyes. There are the stone
teeth, and the breath seeping between them is saying:

"Listen, now. Listen. You are almost here."

Cicadas

1.

Each summer I stretched through the elm tree, tracing
their song, shaking the limbs where they bucked
and chattered, black in that heat
as the black leaves.

I grew, caught only their hulls, dirt
in the husk-beaks, bubbles of lid.

When I was young, I could not understand
where the sound went.

2.

In the 1940's
my uncle was a prisoner in the War.
He lived on his chest and ate grass.
For 38 months and 2 weeks
he said nothing.
When he came home the neighbors said
Fighter. Said Fury. Said Johnny-the-Hero.

It wasn't that, he told me.

He told me the stars over there,
the constellations, were
clustered against the sea.
Each night, when he looked in his one
direction, there was land, then sea, and far
at the end, he said, a little hoop to God.

3.

I grew. He died. One summer I sat
in the moonlight and a brood was climbing,
up through the garden, the elm tree, up
from the roots they had sucked for thirteen

years. Clamped to the bark with their foreclaws,
shivering, splitting at last
through their crisp backs, they pushed

white for that midnight and silent, to their
second lives.
Not redemption. Not souls freed from the body-husk.
Not even endurance.
They just filled that tree to a white
lung, squeezed out in silence
my uncle's mute song:
A thousand opening insects.
Like ice-breath. Like steam.

While You're Away

All year the house has thickened
with neglect: gates scraping
their patterns across the lawn,
knots of bamboo blocking the sky.

I remember that first summer,
the paths we etched through the garden,
the cool, meticulous stones.

Like someone driven I spend these evenings
chopping, clearing. When I sleep
your fine, white body walks toward me.

The Rickers

How does anything start? Here
with the chatter of grackles, the rain-twitched
pines, these stills at our elbows
sucking and wheezing, we shovel a toast
to Ahman, his thin fingers boiling metal,
cooling the vapors to paint—

and paint black on the eyelids,
Cleopatra goggled and grateful, *Al-kuhul, Ahman.*
For the eyes!
Friend we've been grateful since:

Through arrowhead, zeppelin, brigandine,
spat, the slow puckers
of flesh from bone:

Drip and hiss.

Drip and hiss.
We are the rickers, the moonshine colts.
Here, in this cool interference of rain,
we sip, we sip, we sip, we whoop
and the grackles break in their startled splendor,
stroke in the black-winged
splendor, shiver, dip, wink out for the instant
Al-kuhul, boys, al-kuhul! wink
Drink to your warm-blooded hearts.

In Prague, In Montmarte

It is winter in Prague, 1874. On a glass slab,
in a knuckle of sap, chromosomes slip
into focus, for Strasburger, for Flemming,
for the first time. Walther raises his head,
feels in his spine the pull of the hours.
Adolf lowers his head—now the heartrace
thick in his throat: with slow strokes they are
finding each other: helix to helix. Globe.

Just at these moments, in a room in Montmarte,
Degas is tipping his small name to a green pitcher.
And around it, in patches, ballerinas
are drying: cumberbund, anklet, a brushstroke
of shoe. The music has yet to begin.
One woman is scratching her thick back, another
her lip. Row after row, these dancers are clumped
to the wall-rail, awkward, complete in their stillness.

The microscope leans from its thin light.
Excited, now fumbling with joy, Adolf turns
to his friend: Can it be these filaments, these
couple-beads, distinguish us? Nostril? Nail?
This alliance of globes—not fragments, globes?
That the self blossoms from globes?

Degas steps from the canvas, the cumbersome, full
bodies, the music, full, delayed but a moment,
like the dragged note of the milktrain,
just passing—in Prague, in Montmarte—

Yes, he whispers, to no one.

The Asparagus Pickers

The path from the highway
is darker than the fields, chickweed and sorrel
snagging a little night, washing it back
to our ankles and shins.
Oh but the crops are clearing!
A furlong before us, burning its dew,
the long irrigation dolly steams over squat wheels,
stretches its wand halfway across
asparagus troughs. But then, like folly, like
the end of a dream—not water, but a dozen
harnesses sag from the wand: leather,
full-length aprons, to ease

our backaches, our clamping thighs.
Embarrassed, still strangers
fresh in the season, we whisper our thanks to
Apco, to Dunn, to the Yakima Ranches, and enter
the aprons with shallow dives, slip feet
to the booties. The great wand
vibrates above us. The harnesses
shudder. Our tanned hands, looped through
the bodice straps, clutch and shudder. With
a low-pitched moan we are lifted,
a dozen strangers, a foot
from the ground—and the moan echoes as down
the field, eight, ten, eleven dollies
puff and shudder, a hundred bodies, lighter
than water, sway in the crop-steam—there,
and there, as far as the level eye can see:
the shimmering fingers of stalks, the bodies
just over, silent, arboreal,
all the quick joy lifting through.

Anesthesia

—James Young Simpson, 1811-1870

Cows and children nudge in the streets.
There is sunlight, wind. On the roofs the patterns
of thatch and turquoise. And up through it all
the snore of the weaver's shuttle.

Like the dreams you would give us.
James, to sleep on command! To feel
nothing. The tooth, the tumor extracted—there,
just beyond, while the self sits on the tiled rooftops
watching the children.

This, you say, *perhaps this.*
Acetone, benzine, nitrate of oxide of ethel.
It is evening again. Your students, Keith
and Duncan, pay for their suppers with hearty sniffs:
Together, with the motion of cellists, each of you
raises an elbow, breathes from the sweet tumblers.
Keith's eyes grow bright, Duncan waltzes!
And, James, in a tangle of starched cuffs, you
fall to the floor, one after one climb
back to the table, pour chloroform, ether,

stumble, surface.
Plumbing sleep, you laugh. *Plumbing
death. What is there for me but this:
Trial after trial, the wonderful If. . . .*

It is 1869. This morning, near death, you hear
that across the cold Atlantic
the last gold spike
stitches the coast to coast railway.
Propped high in your bed, you see for a moment
two thin boys place their tongues
to the humming track, laugh, watch at eye-level
two lines, then one, then, halfway to Hannibal, a silver
flame. Each rises, straddles
a track beam, slips down as you watch, slips
down and over the rail-line, smaller and smaller,

their tiny bodies bobbing like weights.
You smile, close your eyes, and
James, they are sunlight, they are steam.

Open

Tonight in the clear winter you read
from our table The Book of Dog Breeds,
say Afghan—and I'm off

climbing down from a ship in British
Ceylon, a woman this time or thin man,
abrupt in my jodhpurs. And behind
in cages a cluster of afghans, their
snouts and folk-hair, their billowing
sea legs. Straining now at their leashes,
wheezing, sluicing out through the guava
and scrub—to gather . . . *leopards.*
O those bone-less, long-haired bodies,
black-lipped and yapping, lifting up
through the screw pine like winter steam,
those leopards, churned and climbing,
that island sky, the harbor,

the book, the table, your mouth
saying Bassett, saying Open, saying Pull
from the awe of the eye.

Lesson:
The Spider's Eighth Eye

These three things then: They have eight eyes.
They have memory. Their images do not overlap.

They leave the brood-cocoon when the last grains
of yolk rattle in their pearly bellies.
Each climbs a blade of grass, a twig,
a splintering fence . . . anything sharp and solitary.
Here they send a thread-hook for the wind.

The launch is terrifying: Whipped to a current.
Gusted. Their legs sucked behind, at first,
like so much hair. But somehow they shinney,
and they ride those gossamer V's like arrowheads.

This process—the launch, the travel—this is
called ballooning. Some balloon for days.
They are often found in a ship's rigging,
hundreds of miles from shore.
Or matting an airplane windshield, like cloud-frays.
Those who survive live their lives where the current
drops them. They do not balloon again.

Now, finally, the eyes. They can not converge.
One pair may see you—not as a face, exactly,
but a pale avoidance—just as another sees
the mantel tray, like a gold sun
without heat or shadow.

The eighth eye is tucked below, and has a range
no higher than your knee. It sees only floors,
soil, crackles of plaster. It is the memory eye.
Sometimes when a draft gusts under the door,
or wind whisks the porch, the eighth eye remembers:
It is all very fast—just a spark, in fact:

the wide rush of sea, perhaps a few whales below,
like sun-spots. And then the great flapping
net of a sail.

Of course, the wind should be very brisk.
But since there is memory,
this is how it must be.

Flights of the Harvest-Mare

In Wales, just off from the Radnor Forest,
in the Valley of the Wolves' Jaws,
two women sit in the first sunlight. Far under
their thighs, the globes of their heels, is a circle
of carbon and ash. The women are old, and lean
to each other, feel at their spines the camber and pock
of the answering spine, feel at their palms

the bunch-grass, just over the strata, just
over the ash, where

*nine men have emptied their pockets,
have sliced from the forest the branches of nine
trees. A fire is lighted.
Through the loose lips of burlap bags,
cakes are dropped, oat and brownmeal—*

slowly, without sound—

*as the losers who drop to their knees, having
plucked from the sackcloths the pebbles,
the welts of brownmeal.
Shaking, alone in their thin lines, they will
jump three times through the flames—the oldest,
the weak, landing once, twice in the branch-plumes,
giving up the eyebrows, the hairline, giving
now the ear-flaps, as the great skulls stretch
and plunge,   over   over   over
alive in the fire-skin!*

This is the promise of harvest.

*   *   *

The women lift to their strong shoes, walk
out through the dropband, the steaming ewes. Smoothly,
with the grace-stride of twins, they take
from each other: balance, repair. . . .

We say when wind slips over the grain,
The mare is running! And we reap our tightening
circle, smaller, smaller, to the last tuft
slim in the mulch-field. And that is the Harvest-Mare!
We braid her. We carry her dry
to the ale-house—passed off to each other, out
from our shirt-sleeves, the cuffs of our
leggings—And the women prance with their buckets,
throw fast and again their long
aprons of water.
              But the mare is with us!—
stiff in our clothing, stiff on our calves,
                          and there,
pinned stiff to the roofbeam: the nodding forelock,
the dry shimmering body we drink to.

                    *   *   *

Locked high in the tapered pelvis, the lamb
has buckled.   And the women are singing,
without hesitation, three strong chords
to the churning dam. Just with the low notes,
when the black ears wither and flap
a hand is slipped through the lips of the vulva.
Sucked to the wrist, the forearm, it nudges at last,
deep in the birthpath, the skull and tangled
hooves, circles the nape, the chest-bridge,
pulls from the sucking, turns, pulls
to that first sunlight, the muzzle, two small hooves
like a diver.

Now the woman
raises her slick hand, addresses
the hillsides, the valley, the other
so long her companion.
She waits, laughing, while the muzzle
is cleared.
            And now, as the lamb stammers
its first sound, she will drop her hand,
will feel through her breasts, for an
instant, the flow, the course and withdrawal

of song. *What we cannot control, we control,* she will say.

When very young, Linda Bierds moved with her family from her birth-place, Wilmington, Delaware, to Anchorage, Alaska, where she lived until she was seven years old. Since then, she has lived in Seattle, Washington. She earned a B.A. and an M.A. in Creative Writing from the University of Washington, and she now edits the publications of the Women's Information Center at that school. She also teaches poetry in the schools under the auspices of the Washington State Arts Commission. Her work as a docent at Seattle's Woodland Park Zoo reflects her interest in animals, endangered species in particular. She has published poetry in over sixty magazines, including, most recently, **The New England Review**, **The Massachusetts Review**, *and* **The New Yorker**.

Ahsahta Press

POETRY OF THE WEST

MODERN

*Norman Macleod, *Selected Poems*
Gwendolen Haste, *Selected Poems*
*Peggy Pond Church, *New & Selected Poems*
Haniel Long, *My Seasons*
H. L. Davis, *Selected Poems*
*Hildegarde Flanner, *The Hearkening Eye*
Genevieve Taggard, *To the Natural World*
Hazel Hall, *Selected Poems*
Women Poets of the West: An Anthology
*Thomas Hornsby Ferril, *Anvil of Roses*
*Judson Crews, *The Clock of Moss*

CONTEMPORARY

*Marnie Walsh, *A Taste of the Knife*
*Robert Krieger, *Headlands, Rising*
Richard Blessing, *Winter Constellations*
*Carolyne Wright, *Stealing the Children*
Charley John Greasybear, *Songs*
*Conger Beasley, Jr., *Over DeSoto's Bones*
*Susan Strayer Deal, *No Moving Parts*
*Gretel Ehrlich, *To Touch the Water*
*Leo Romero, *Agua Negra*
*David Baker, *Laws of the Land*
*Richard Speakes, *Hannah's Travel*
Dixie Partridge, *Deer in the Haystacks*
Philip St. Clair, *At the Tent of Heaven*
Susan Strayer Deal, *The Dark Is a Door*
Linda Bierds, *Flights of the Harvest-Mare*

*Selections from these volumes, read by their authors, are now available
on *The Ahsahta Cassette Sampler.*